American Moments

ABDO
Daughters

THE ASSASSINATION
OF JOHN F. KENNEDY

By Sheila Rivera

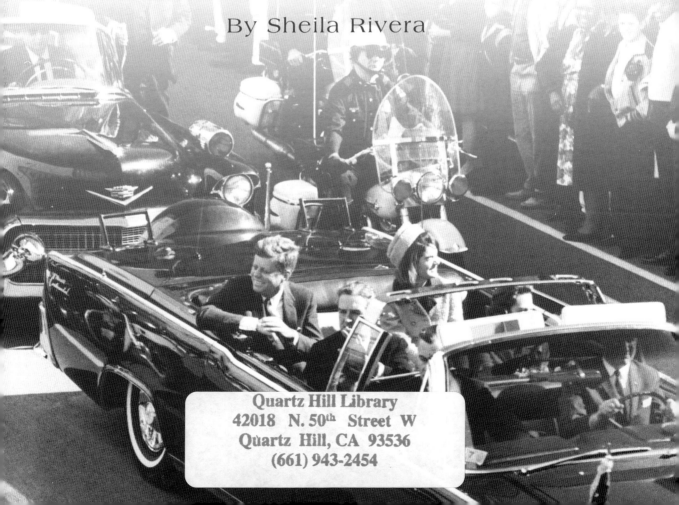

VISIT US AT
WWW.ABDOPUB.COM

Published by ABDO Publishing Company, 4940 Viking Drive, Suite 622, Edina, Minnesota 55435. Copyright ©2004 by Abdo Consulting Group, Inc. International copyrights reserved in all countries. No part of this book may be reproduced in any form without written permission from the publisher.

Printed in the United States.

Edited by: Cory Gunderson
Contributing Editor: Tamara L. Britton
Cover Design: Mighty Media
Interior Design and Production: Terry Dunham Incorporated
Photos: Corbis, Library of Congress

Library of Congress Cataloging-in-Publication Data

Rivera, Sheila, 1970-
   The assassination of John F. Kennedy / Sheila Rivera.
     p. cm. -- (American moments)
  Summary: A look at the people, events, and controversy involved in the assassination of President John F. Kennedy in 1963.
  Includes bibliographical references (p.) and index.
  ISBN 1-59197-277-9
   1. Kennedy, John F. (John Fitzgerald), 1917-1963--Assassination--Juvenile literature. [1. Kennedy, John F. (John Fitzgerald), 1917-1963--Assassination.] I. Title. II. Series.

E842.9R56 2003
973.922'092--dc21
[B]

2003044340

CONTENTS

American Moments

THE LIFE OF JOHN F. KENNEDY

John Fitzgerald Kennedy was born on May 29, 1917, in Brookline, Massachusetts. His parents were Joseph Patrick Kennedy and Rose Fitzgerald. Joseph Patrick Kennedy was a multimillionaire. He made money in the banking, shipbuilding, and motion picture industries, as well as in the stock market. Rose Fitzgerald was the daughter of former Boston mayor John F. Fitzgerald.

John F. Kennedy was the second of nine children. His brothers and sisters were Joseph Patrick Jr., Rosemary, Kathleen, Eunice, Patricia, Robert, Jean, and Edward.

As a child, Kennedy attended private schools. In high school, he was voted most likely to succeed. During the summer of 1935, at the age of 18, he went to England. There he studied at the London School of Economics. Kennedy returned to the United States at the end of the summer. He began studying at Princeton University that fall.

Kennedy was forced to leave Princeton during his first year of college. He suffered from a severe case of jaundice. Jaundice is a sickness that causes a person's skin to appear yellow. Doctors struggled to find the source of Kennedy's illness. As an adult, he would be diagnosed with Addison's disease. But at this time, his sickness was a mystery, and soon he was feeling much better.

In 1936, Kennedy entered Harvard University. He graduated with honors in 1940. Before graduating, Kennedy wrote a paper on British military policy in the 1930s. Later he published this paper as a book. It was titled *Why England Slept*. It was a best seller. As a young man, Kennedy enjoyed writing. His desire was to become a journalist.

In the spring of 1941, countries all over the world were fighting in World War II. Kennedy volunteered for the army. He was rejected because he had a weak back. He had injured his back while playing sports in college. But Kennedy was not discouraged. During the summer, he did strengthening exercises to improve his health. His goal was to eventually enter the military. In September, he joined the navy.

In March 1943, Kennedy became the commander of a torpedo boat in the Solomon Islands. It was called *PT109*. On August 2 of that year, *PT109* was rammed and sunk by a Japanese ship. Kennedy worked heroically to save his crew and get them to land. They swam three miles (5 km) to a nearby island.

The Purple Heart

John F. Kennedy received a Purple Heart for his actions in the Solomon Islands. The Purple Heart is awarded to men and women who are wounded or killed while performing military service. This award was created by the first U.S. president, George Washington.

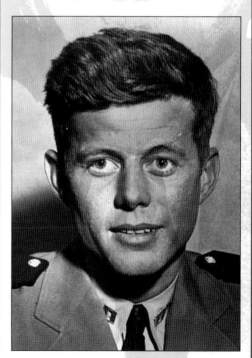

John F. Kennedy served in the navy from 1941 to 1945.

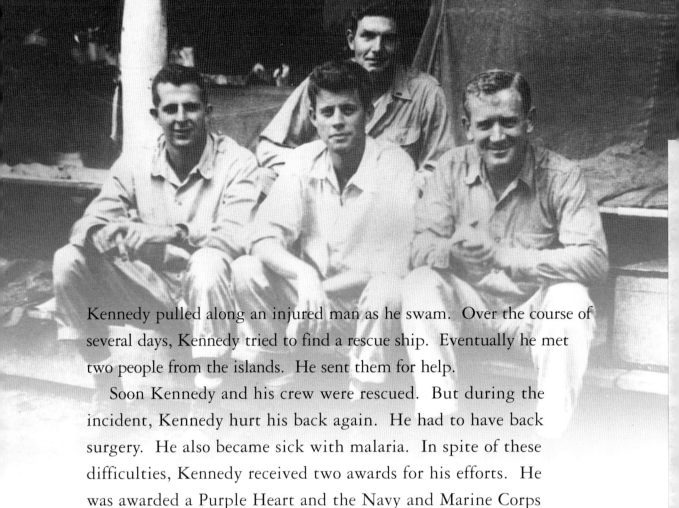

Kennedy pulled along an injured man as he swam. Over the course of several days, Kennedy tried to find a rescue ship. Eventually he met two people from the islands. He sent them for help.

Soon Kennedy and his crew were rescued. But during the incident, Kennedy hurt his back again. He had to have back surgery. He also became sick with malaria. In spite of these difficulties, Kennedy received two awards for his efforts. He was awarded a Purple Heart and the Navy and Marine Corps Medal for heroism. He was discharged from the navy in 1945.

After his military career ended, Kennedy worked as a journalist. For several months in 1945, he was a reporter for Hearst Newspapers. One of his big stories was about the conference in San Francisco, California, to establish the United Nations.

But a life as a journalist was not to be. Influenced by his father, Kennedy chose a career in politics. In 1946, Representative James M. Curley left the House of Representatives. Curley's seat in the House was vacant, and Kennedy decided to pursue it. In early 1946, Kennedy announced that he would run in the Democratic primary election that June.

Kennedy campaigned vigorously. He ran against nine other

Top of page: *John F. Kennedy and crew members in the Solomon Islands* candidates who also wanted the seat. One of the candidates called Kennedy "the poor, little rich kid." Others referred to him as an outsider.

Kennedy was not always popular within the Democratic Party. He did not depend on regular Democratic Party workers in his campaign. He was supported by a strong group of family and friends.

In the June primary election, Kennedy won almost double the votes of his nearest opponent. In November, the people of Massachusetts elected Kennedy to the House of Representatives. Kennedy was elected to a second term in 1948. He was reelected again in 1950.

As a representative, Kennedy voted for laws that helped common people. He favored low-cost public housing and health care. He agreed with many of President Harry Truman's foreign policies. Yet, he felt that the president's stand against communism was weak. Kennedy supported a strong anticommunist foreign policy throughout his political career.

In April 1952, Kennedy announced that he would run for a seat in the Senate. He ran against incumbent Republican

The donkey became associated with the Democratic Party in 1828 when Andrew Jackson ran for the presidency.

Democrats regard the donkey as humble, smart, courageous, and lovable.

Although the donkey is often associated with the Democratic Party, it has never been formally adopted as the party's symbol.

Henry Cabot Lodge Jr. Again, Kennedy relied on his family and friends during his campaign. His slogan was, "Kennedy will do more for Massachusetts." Kennedy won the November election by more than 70,000 votes. He became the junior senator from Massachusetts.

On September 12, 1953, Kennedy married Jacqueline Bouvier. She was often called Jackie. Jackie was born on July 28, 1929. Her parents were Janet Lee Bouvier and John Vernon Bouvier III. After high school, Jackie went to Vassar College. During her junior year, she studied in Paris, France. Jackie returned to the United States and graduated from George Washington University in Washington DC.

John and Jackie's marriage was a huge social event. About 1,300 guests attended the reception. Jackie did not have experience in politics, but she was supportive of her husband's career. She helped Kennedy with his public speaking.

John and Jackie cut their wedding cake.

John and Jackie Kennedy would have three children. Their daughter, Caroline Bouvier Kennedy, was born on November 27, 1957. Their son, John F. Kennedy Jr., was born on November 25, 1960. The Kennedys' third child, a son named Patrick Bouvier Kennedy, was born on August 7, 1963. He died only two days later.

After his marriage, Kennedy returned to work in the Senate. However, he continued to have back problems. He had back surgery in 1954 and again in 1955. While he was recovering, he wrote another book, *Profiles in Courage*. It was about eight U.S. senators. The book won a Pulitzer Prize for biography in 1957.

When he returned to the Senate, Kennedy fought for civil rights. He supported desegregation of schools. He also helped arrange a compromise on a civil rights bill in 1957.

In 1958, Kennedy ran for reelection to the Senate. Kennedy's popularity helped him win the election by more than 874,000 votes. This made him a good candidate for the next presidential election.

In January 1960, Kennedy announced that he would run for president. Once again his family and friends ran his campaign. He beat Minnesota senator Hubert H. Humphrey Jr. and others in the primary election. He was nominated to be the Democrats' candidate for president on the first ballot at the Democratic national convention. Kennedy accepted the nomination. He declared, "We stand today on the edge of a New Frontier." This became the theme of his campaign.

Kennedy ran for president against Republican candidate Richard M. Nixon. Nixon was vice president at the time. The two men participated in a series of televised debates. Political candidates had never debated on television before.

On television, Kennedy looked good. Many Republicans thought Kennedy was too young to run for president. They had felt he was not experienced enough to hold such a high office. But his mature appearance and enthusiastic speech gained him much public support. During the debates, Kennedy promised new health, housing, and civil rights programs. He pledged that his New Frontier would help the country's economy.

When Kennedy and Nixon participated in their historic televised debate, television was a recent invention. Televisions were expensive, and few families owned one. So most people listened to the debate on radio.

Radio listeners could not see the candidates. They could only concentrate on the debate. Many radio listeners thought Nixon had won.

Television viewers had more to focus on than the debate. They could see Nixon's nervousness and Kennedy's calm confidence. Most television viewers thought Kennedy had won.

This debate not only ushered in the era of televised political debate, but also demonstrated how television could manipulate public opinion.

Richard Nixon did not fare as well in the televised debates. He wore heavy makeup. And the hot lights in the television studio made him sweaty. Nixon's poor appearance improved the public's perception of Kennedy.

Nearly 69 million people voted in the election. Kennedy won the popular vote by only 119,450 votes. However, he won 303 electoral votes, while Nixon received only 219. Kennedy became the first Roman Catholic president of the United States. At the age of 43, he was also the youngest elected president. His running mate Lyndon B. Johnson became vice president.

John F. Kennedy was sworn in on January 20, 1961. In his inaugural speech, he made his famous statement, "Ask not what your country can do for you; ask what you can do for your country." He promised to fight what he called "the common enemies of man: tyranny, poverty, disease, and war itself."

As First Lady, Jackie Kennedy wanted the White House to be a place where her children could grow up comfortably and the family could have privacy. Jackie also saw the White House as a historical building. She wanted it to reflect U.S. history. To this end, she created the White House Historical Society.

With the help of that group, she worked to redecorate the White House. Jackie supervised a White House tour, which was filmed for the public. It was shown on television on Valentine's Day in 1962. Its broadcast reached 106 countries worldwide. The young Kennedy family brought new energy to the White House. They often invited artists, writers, scientists, musicians, actors, and athletes to visit.

As president, Kennedy faced several international crises. His role in these events affected how Americans felt about him. His first international challenge was the Bay of Pigs invasion.

Fidel Castro had been Cuba's leader since 1959. He ruled Cuba under a communist system of government. Over time, Castro gained a lot of power. He took over U.S. businesses there. Many Cuban people were unhappy with Castro's strict government. Thousands of Cubans left the country.

These actions strained the relationship between Cuba and the United States. Tension was also growing between the United States and the Union of Soviet Socialist Republics, also called the Soviet Union. Like Cuba, the Soviet Union was a communist country. Cuba and the Soviet Union had developed close ties. The United States feared the possibility of a Soviet-influenced communist invasion from Cuba. Cuba is only 90 miles (145 km) from the Florida coast. To avoid this, the U.S. government decided to lead its own invasion into Cuba. The goal was to rid Cuba of Castro, and free the Cuban citizens from communist control.

The Central Intelligence Agency (CIA) urged Cuban exiles to rise up against Castro.

FIDEL CASTRO

After the failed Bay of Pigs invasion, U.S. intelligence forces were said to have plotted the assassination of Cuban leader Fidel Castro. Some of their ideas included: poison cigars, a mafia contract, a deadly wet suit, and an exploding seashell.

Fidel Castro

Bay of Pigs

CUBA

With U.S. support, the CIA thought the Cubans would be able to overthrow Castro's communist government.

The United States spent more than $46 million on the invasion. It spent the money on political action, propaganda, weapons, training, and information gathering. Inside Cuba, newspapers and radio stations reported anti-Castro messages. Outside of Cuba, the U.S. military trained Cuban exiles. They gathered in the Central American nations of Guatemala and Nicaragua.

On April 17, 1961, troops invaded Cuba at the Bay of Pigs. But Castro was expecting them. Castro's military overtook the forces. Within three days, the invasion was over. Soon, U.S. involvement in the invasion became widely known. Its failure was embarrassing to President Kennedy.

The United States was not able to overthrow Cuba's communist government. So Kennedy decided to apply political and economic pressure to topple the government. The U.S. government banned Cuban exports from entering the United States. It also cut off all diplomatic communication with Cuba.

The Bay of Pigs invasion had barely ended when the second important international event of Kennedy's administration began. In June 1961, Kennedy met with Soviet premier Nikita Khrushchev in Vienna, Austria. They met to talk about the rising tension between the governments of East and West Germany.

After World War II, Germany had been divided into two countries. East Germany had a communist government. West Germany had a democratic government. The line that separated the two nations ran through the city of Berlin. Allied forces stationed in West Berlin guarded against communist invasion from the east.

Kennedy did not agree with the ideas of communism. He fought against communist influence in Europe and North America. Kennedy pledged his support to West Germany. Khrushchev did not like Kennedy's democratic ideas. He threatened to sign a peace treaty with East Germany. This treaty would end the allied presence in West Berlin.

Kennedy stood strong in defense of West Germany. Eventually the Soviets backed down. They did not sign the treaty with East Germany. Instead, Khrushchev ordered them to build a wall in Berlin along the border of the two countries. It was called the Berlin wall. The purpose of the wall was to keep people from escaping from East Germany and going to West Germany.

President Kennedy was not pleased with the Berlin wall. Tensions continued to build between the United States and the Soviet Union. By 1962, both countries had nuclear weapons. Each country felt threatened by the other. They both continued building more and more nuclear weapons. Each country felt that if it had the most weapons the other country would be too afraid to attack.

The west side of the Berlin wall

That same year, Kennedy claimed that the Soviet Union had more missiles than the United States had. The truth was just the opposite. To make up for the difference, Soviet premier Khrushchev began secretly moving nuclear missiles from the Soviet Union to Cuba. This would make it easier to strike targets in the United States.

In October, the U.S. government sent spy aircraft to fly over Cuba. From the spy aircraft, officials saw the weapons that the Soviet Union had moved to Cuba. They took pictures of the weapons from the airplane. This was the beginning of what came to be known as the Cuban missile crisis.

President Kennedy's military advisers wanted to destroy the Soviet missiles in Cuba. The advisers wanted to drop bombs on

During the Cuban missile crisis, U.S. officials used photos taken from planes flying over Cuba to monitor missile launch sites.

the missiles. Kennedy did not allow them to do this. He would not order an invasion of Cuba either. He thought that if the United States took military action, the Soviets would attack West Berlin. In addition, Kennedy's secretary of defense believed that if the United States took military action it might lead to a world war.

Instead of attacking Cuba, Kennedy ordered a naval blockade. U.S. warships surrounded the island. They stopped any ships from carrying weapons or oil to Cuba. Khrushchev could see that the Soviet Union was at a disadvantage. If it took military action against the United States, it would have to supply an army halfway around the world.

Khrushchev and Kennedy met to discuss a solution to the crisis. Khrushchev agreed to remove the missiles from Cuba. Kennedy promised that the United States would not invade Cuba. He also promised to remove U.S. missiles that were in place in Turkey as an even trade. Both Kennedy and Khrushchev agreed to keep the deal a secret, and the crisis ended.

On November 20, the United States ended the blockade. Soviet bombers and missiles left Cuba by the end of the year. The quiet end to the crisis made it look like the United States had won. The truth that both sides reached a compromise was not made public until years later.

As he worked to solve national security problems, President Kennedy also addressed issues within the United States. One issue that he took a firm stand on was civil rights. During the 1960s, there was a lot of discrimination against African Americans in the United States. Kennedy felt that blacks and whites should have equal opportunities. In his campaign speeches, Kennedy had promised to act swiftly to help African Americans.

In 1960, the Civil Rights Commission had released a report. It showed that 57 percent of African Americans lived in housing that was unacceptable. African-American life expectancy was seven years less than that of white Americans. The infant mortality rate was twice as high for African Americans as it was for whites.

To address these issues, Kennedy urged the federal government to hire more African Americans. Kennedy gave many African Americans public posts. He appointed 40 African Americans to high-status federal jobs. Five became federal judges.

In his fight for civil rights, Kennedy created the Committee on Equal Employment Opportunity, or CEEO. It ensured that all people who worked for the federal government had equal job opportunities. It required all companies that had contracts with the federal government to offer equal job opportunities to their employees, too. If they did not, they would not get new contracts. The CEEO only helped people who were already employed.

Kennedy appointed his brother, Robert F. Kennedy, to the office of U.S. attorney general. This made Robert Kennedy the head of the Department of Justice. The two brothers used the courts to enforce civil rights laws.

President Kennedy and Robert Kennedy had a close working relationship. It was very successful. Robert Kennedy had directed the president's 1952 Senate campaign. He also managed President Kennedy's presidential campaign in 1960. Robert Kennedy was a strong political adviser. The president trusted his brother more than anyone else.

After the Bay of Pigs invasion, Robert Kennedy advised President Kennedy on top-secret matters. He helped with international agreements as well. His advice during the Cuban missile crisis helped it reach its peaceful conclusion.

Robert F. Kennedy

THE ASSASSINATION

On November 22, 1963, President Kennedy and his supporters were traveling in a motorcade in Dallas, Texas. Kennedy was visiting Texas to gain public support for his candidacy in the next presidential election. Besides Dallas, the president's trip to Texas also included stops in San Antonio, Houston, and Fort Worth.

The motorcade in which the president rode contained many vehicles. At the front were four police officers on motorcycles and a lead car. The first car carried the Dallas police chief and U.S. Secret Service agents. The president's car followed. President Kennedy, Jackie, Texas governor John B. Connally, and his wife Nellie rode together in a seven-passenger convertible. The car traveled through the streets with its top down. Kennedy didn't like the protective bubbletop that could have been used on the car. He wanted the people to be able to see him and his wife.

John F. Kennedy in his motorcade

In the front seats of the president's car were two Secret Service agents. Governor Connally and his wife sat in the next seats. President Kennedy and the First Lady sat behind Governor and Mrs. Connally. On each side of the car were motorcycle escorts. President Kennedy did not want them beside the car because he felt it looked bad. But they needed to be there to protect him.

Following the president's car was another car. It carried more Secret Service agents. Vice President Johnson's car was next in line. In it were Vice President Johnson, his wife Lady Bird, Senator Ralph Yarborough, and other security staff. Most of the cars in the motorcade held security agents and officers.

Before Kennedy's arrival, Dallas newspapers printed the route that the motorcade would travel. It was published on November 18 and 19, just days before his arrival. This information allowed people to plan where to go so they could see the president. However, it also showed potential assassins where the president would be.

NOVEMBER 22, 1963

11:40 AM
President Kennedy and his party arrive in Dallas, Texas.

11:50 AM
Kennedy's motorcade begins its journey through Dallas neighborhoods.

12:30 PM
Kennedy is shot.

12:34 PM
Dallas police suggest shots came from the Texas School Book Depository Building.

12:45 PM
Police release a description of the suspected shooter.

1:00 PM
Kennedy is pronounced dead.

1:55 PM
Police arrest Lee Harvey Oswald.

2:38 PM
Vice President Lyndon B. Johnson is sworn in as president aboard *Air Force One.*

Dealey Plaza

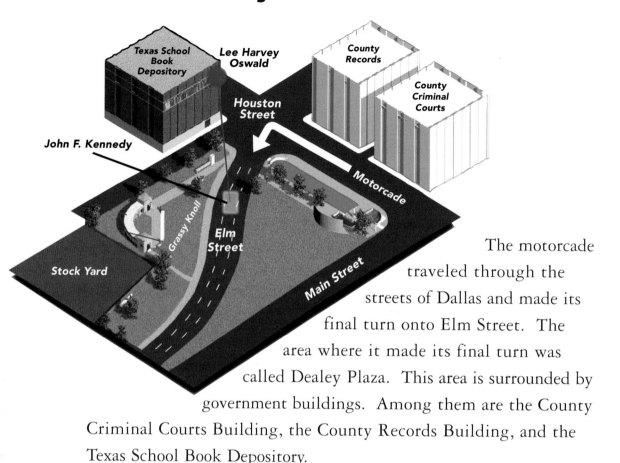

The motorcade traveled through the streets of Dallas and made its final turn onto Elm Street. The area where it made its final turn was called Dealey Plaza. This area is surrounded by government buildings. Among them are the County Criminal Courts Building, the County Records Building, and the Texas School Book Depository.

There is a hill in Dealey Plaza known as the grassy knoll. Many people stood there to watch the president's motorcade. As the president's car approached the grassy knoll, Governor Connally's wife said to Kennedy, "Mr. President, you can't say Dallas doesn't love you." He responded with a smile.

As the president's car passed the grassy knoll, several shots rang out. Both President Kennedy and Governor Connally were shot. People panicked. Some of the people watching the motorcade dove to the ground. Others ran for cover. Secret Service agents ran from the other vehicles to surround and protect the president. A Secret Service agent named Clint Hill was one of the first agents to get to the president's car. A bullet hit the president's head before agent Hill could protect him. In a panic, Mrs. Kennedy tried to climb out onto the trunk of the car.

The president and governor were rushed to Parkland Memorial Hospital. President Kennedy was pronounced dead at 1:00 PM. Governor Connally was hurt, but he survived.

Vice President Johnson and Jackie rode with the president's body to *Air Force One*, the presidential airplane. Before the plane took off to return to Washington DC, Johnson was sworn in as president of the United States.

The news of President Kennedy's death spread quickly. World leaders called U.S. officials at the White House and aboard *Air Force One* to offer their sympathy.

Shortly after arriving in Washington DC, the newly sworn in President Johnson made a statement to the media. He said, "We have suffered a loss that cannot be weighed. For me it is a personal tragedy. I will do my best. That is all I can do." The whole nation mourned with Jackie, Caroline, and John Jr. President Kennedy was only 46 years old when he was killed.

With Jacqueline Kennedy at his side, Lyndon B. Johnson is sworn in as president.

THE
ASSASSIN

Immediately, the people in Dealey Plaza began to look for the shooter. Witnesses and police officers ran up the grassy knoll. They looked behind the wooden fence that ran behind it. Other officers searched the underpass beneath a nearby bridge.

Several witnesses came forth with clues. A 16-year-old boy named Amos Euins told police that he had seen someone with a gun in the window of the Texas School Book Depository. Another witness, Howard Brennan, had also seen the person. Brennan described him as a thin, white man in his early 30s.

One of the police officers who had been in the motorcade, Marrion Baker, was already at the depository. He was sure that the gunshots had come from there. He had jumped off his motorcycle and run inside just seconds after the president was shot.

Officer Baker and the building manager, Roy Truly, ran inside and up the stairs. On the second floor, Officer Baker confronted a man who was entering the lunchroom. This was only about two minutes after the shooting, but the man was not out of breath, and he was not carrying a weapon. Baker asked Truly if he knew the man. Truly answered, "Yes, he works for me." Baker and Truly left the lunchroom and went up to the fifth floor. From the fifth floor, they took the elevator to the

The rifle suspected of being used to kill John F. Kennedy

24

seventh floor, and then to the roof.

Once Baker and Truly left the lunchroom, the man they had seen left the building. He was 24-year-old Lee Harvey Oswald. About 40 minutes later, Oswald was seen going into the rooming house where he lived. He left soon afterward.

The window from which Lee Harvey Oswald shot John F. Kennedy

The Texas School Book Depository

Police broadcast a description of the suspect from the book depository to all patrol cars in the area. Officer John Tippit was driving through a residential neighborhood when he saw a man who fit the description. Tippit stopped his car and got out. The man fired five shots at the officer with a revolver. The man took the bullet casings out of the gun and threw them into some weedy grass. He reloaded the gun and marched off down the street. Another man witnessed the shooting and used the radio in the police car to call for help. Police broadcast a description of this gunman to other officers. An officer responded right away. He said he had seen someone fitting the description run into the public library. But the person turned out to be a library employee who had run into the building to tell his friends about the president's assassination. He was not the shooter.

Several blocks away a shop manager, Johnny Brewer, was listening to the radio news broadcast. He heard about the officer

25

who had been shot nearby. He saw a man walk by his store. He noticed that every time a police car passed, the man would turn to hide his face. Brewer went outside. He saw the man go into the Texas Theater.

Brewer told a theater employee about the suspicious man. They called the police. Within minutes, police surrounded the building. Inside the theater, Brewer pointed out the man. The police lined up everyone in the theater to be searched.

Officer Nick McDonald began checking the man that Brewer pointed out. He approached the man and said, "Get on your feet." The man replied, "Well, it's all over now." He jumped up and punched the officer between the eyes. At the same time, he drew a gun from the waist of his pants.

Officer McDonald hit the man back. He and three other officers wrestled the man to the ground. They handcuffed him, dragged him outside, and put him in a patrol car parked outside the theater. The man tried to defend himself by saying, "The only thing I have done is carry a pistol in a movie." One of the officers replied, "You've done a lot more, you've killed a policeman."

At police headquarters, detective Gus Rose helped interview the man. Rose looked through the man's wallet. Inside he found identification cards with two different names on them. One had the name Lee Harvey Oswald. Another said Alek Hidell. Rose asked the man if he was Oswald or Hidell. The man replied, "You find out."

Just then Captain Fritz entered. He told Rose to find an employee of the Texas School Book Depository. The employee's name was Lee Harvey Oswald. Rose was stunned. He told the captain that they already had Oswald. Over the next two days they questioned Oswald intensively.

Opposite page: *Lee Harvey Oswald was arrested in New Orleans in 1963 for disturbing the peace.*

Lee Harvey Oswald was born in New Orleans, Louisiana, on October 18, 1939. His parents were Marguerite Francis Claverie and Robert Edward Lee Oswald. The Oswald family moved to Dallas in 1944. As a boy, Oswald was an average student. People described him as shy, and a loner. In high school, he was often in trouble for fighting or other disciplinary problems.

When Oswald was 17 years old, he joined the U.S. Marine Corps. In the marines, he was trained to shoot an M-1 rifle. He also worked as a radar operator. In 1958, he was court-martialed for having an unregistered gun in his living quarters. The gun was discovered when Oswald accidentally shot himself in the elbow. He was court-martialed again that year for disobeying a sergeant.

While he was in the marines, Oswald became interested in the Soviet Union and communism. He began studying the Russian language. In 1959, Oswald was honorably discharged from the marines. This means that he left the marines on good terms. He then joined the U.S. Marine Corps Reserves.

In October 1960, Oswald moved to the Soviet Union. A year later, Oswald was dishonorably discharged from the Marine Corps Reserves. He was dismissed for giving up his U.S. citizenship.

NEW ORLEANS, LA.

After two years in the Soviet Union, Oswald became unhappy with his new country. In 1962, he returned to the United States with his Soviet-born wife, Marina, and their baby daughter, June.

In the United States, Oswald joined a group called the Fair Play for Cuba Committee. He supported the Castro government. He began planning a trip to Cuba. Throughout the summer of 1963, Oswald printed fliers and staged demonstrations in support of Castro. In November, he was charged with shooting President John F. Kennedy, Governor John B. Connally, and police officer John Tippit.

On November 23, 1963, the local Federal Bureau of Investigation (FBI) received an anonymous phone call. The caller said that a group of men was going to try to kill Oswald the next morning when he was moved from the police station to the county jail. This made some officials wonder if Oswald should be moved in secret. Dallas police decided to drive Oswald to the county jail in an armored truck.

On the morning of November 24, Captain Fritz changed his mind about using the armored truck. He decided that Oswald would be moved in a car instead. The transfer was scheduled for 10:00 AM. It wasn't until after 11:00 AM that police began the process. Oswald insisted on wearing a disguise. He said that everyone knew what clothes he was wearing because of all the media attention he'd gotten. The police gave Oswald an old, black sweater to wear.

Outside the police station, more than 70 police officers and 40 reporters waited. Detectives brought Oswald out into a basement parking area. They led him past the waiting reporters. Television cameras were to broadcast Oswald's transfer live across the nation. Suddenly, a man stepped out from the crowd. He pulled out a gun and shot Oswald in the abdomen. Oswald collapsed to the ground. Detectives immediately arrested the shooter. He was later identified as Jack Ruby.

Officers pulled Oswald back into the building and called an ambulance. He was rushed to Parkland Memorial Hospital. At 1:07 PM, Oswald was pronounced dead. Captain Fritz later said, "I have always felt it was Ruby who made the [anonymous] call." Both Lee Harvey Oswald and President John F. Kennedy were buried the same day.

Jack Ruby went to court and was found guilty of murdering Lee Harvey Oswald. He was sentenced to death. Ruby's lawyer appealed his case. However, Ruby had cancer, and he died before he could be granted a new trial.

Jack Ruby's killing of Lee Harvey Oswald hindered the investigation into President Kennedy's assassination. With Oswald dead, it would be nearly impossible for law enforcement agents to know for sure if he really was the president's killer.

KENNEDY'S FUNERAL

When President Kennedy died, U.S. citizens mourned the death of their leader. The president's body was returned to Washington DC from Dallas. It was placed in the East Room of the White House. Jackie chose this room because it was where President Lincoln's body was placed after he was assassinated in 1865.

Two hours before dawn on November 23, 1963, the White House staff attended a service for Kennedy. People across the nation held their own memorials for the president. The following morning, Jackie and Robert Kennedy went to the East Room to see the president's body for the last time. Jackie placed three letters inside Kennedy's casket. One she had written herself. The other two were from John Jr. and Caroline. John Jr.'s letter was only scribbles. Jackie also placed two of her husband's favorite possessions in the casket. The first was a pair of gold cuff links. The second was a carving with the presidential seal on it. The casket was closed and brought outside.

President Kennedy's casket was carried to the Capitol on a two-wheeled cart called a caisson. It was pulled by a team of white horses. A black, riderless horse was led through the procession. Thousands of people lined the streets of Washington DC, silently watching. People outside of Washington DC watched the procession on television.

John F. Kennedy Jr. salutes his father's casket.

Once the procession reached the Capitol, military officers fired a 21-gun salute to honor the president. Pallbearers carried the casket up to the Capitol Rotunda. This is the dome-shaped area inside the Capitol. The U.S. Navy Band played *Hail to the Chief*.

The Kennedy family and several government officials paid their last respects to the president. Then an honor guard surrounded the casket, and the rotunda was opened to the public. Thousands of people came to bid farewell to the president. The line was so long it took people hours to reach the casket. They came all afternoon and into the evening.

The next day, President Kennedy was buried in Arlington National Cemetery in Virginia. Kennedy's funeral procession began at 9:45 AM. His casket was carried back down the steps of the Capitol Rotunda and placed on the caisson. It was carried to St. Matthew's Cathedral. Television stations worldwide broadcast the procession. It was even shown in the Soviet Union.

A funeral was held at the cathedral. Afterward, the casket was placed back on the caisson for its final trip to Arlington National Cemetery. The Kennedy family and other important people followed the caisson in black limousines.

At the cemetery, the U.S. Marine Band played the *Star-Spangled Banner*, and a Scottish bagpipe group played *Mist-Covered Mountain*. A fleet of 49 jets flew over as Kennedy's body was placed into the grave. One plane was missing. This symbolized Kennedy's death. Then *Air Force One* flew by and tipped its wings as a tribute to the president. The group prayed, then military officers fired a 21-gun salute. Finally, a bugler played *Taps*. The flag that had covered the casket was given to Mrs. Kennedy. Then she lit the eternal flame that was constructed at Kennedy's grave site. This flame still burns in his honor today.

Opposite page: *Kennedy's funeral procession*

THE WARREN COMMISSION INVESTIGATES

The American people wanted answers to the questions surrounding President Kennedy's death. They wanted to know if Oswald had acted alone when he killed the president. Because of Oswald's death, their questions went unanswered. The people turned to President Lyndon B. Johnson.

President Johnson formed a committee to investigate Kennedy's death. The group was the Warren Commission, named after one of the group's members, Chief Justice Earl Warren. The other members of the Warren Commission were senators, state representatives, and lawyers.

President Johnson told the commission to look at all the facts and circumstances surrounding Kennedy's death. He ordered them to examine the circumstances surrounding Oswald's killing as well. He wanted them to find out if the president's killing had been directed or encouraged by anyone. He told the group to create a report of its findings and conclusions and report back to him.

The Warren Commission's investigation lasted ten months. It gathered information from the CIA, the FBI, and the Secret Service. At the end of its investigation, the commission gave President Johnson an 888-page report. It contained 26 volumes of evidence and conclusions.

Warren Commission members (left to right):
Gerald Ford, Hale Boggs, Richard Russell, Earl Warren,
John Cooper, John McCloy, Allen Dulles, and Lee Rankin

The first chapter of the report contained the commission's basic findings and conclusions. After that was a detailed analysis of the facts surrounding the events of November 22, 1963, and the two days that followed. Other chapters covered the following topics: the trip to Dallas, the shots fired from the Texas School Book Depository, the killer's identity, the murder of Lee Harvey Oswald, the possibility that there was a conspiracy against the president, Oswald's background and possible motive, and arrangements for the president's protection. Based on the evidence it collected, the commission concluded that Lee Harvey Oswald was President Kennedy's assassin.

CONSPIRACY THEORIES

Although Oswald was charged with Kennedy's murder, many people did not believe that he acted alone. Some people doubted that one person could have been so successful in shooting and killing the president. Witnesses' reports made the original explanation seem impossible. The public demanded to know the truth. People wanted to know if Oswald had been part of a conspiracy to kill John F. Kennedy.

Some of the people interviewed by the Warren Commission reported hearing up to four gunshots. This differs from the official report of three shots. The shots seemed to have varying degrees of loudness, too. This suggests that they may have been fired from more than one location.

Several witnesses said that they heard shots coming from the grassy knoll, not from the direction of the book depository. One person who said this was a Secret Service agent.

Agent Paul Landis had been riding in the car behind the president's car at the time of the shooting. He told the commission, "I still was not certain from which direction the second shot came, but my reaction at this time was that the shot came from somewhere toward the front, right-hand side of the road." This was the opposite direction of the book depository.

People also wondered if Oswald had a strong enough reason to kill the president. Oswald supported Cuba. He might have been angry with the president for his position against Fidel Castro and Cuba's communist government. It seemed likely, however, that another person or group might have had a stronger reason than Oswald to want the president dead.

One possibility was that the Cuban government was behind the killing. After all, the United States and Cuba had been at odds just before Kennedy's death. The Cuban government was said to be angry about a CIA plot to kill Castro. It may have planned to kill Kennedy in return.

Others said that the mafia might have been responsible. The mafia is a secret criminal organization. Robert Kennedy had been working against crime leaders. There were secretly taped conversations of mafia leaders saying that they wanted President Kennedy dead.

With all of these factors in the open, the truth about the murder was unclear. The Warren Commission laid out the case against Oswald, but the nation was not completely convinced.

In September 1976, another group was created to investigate assassinations. It was called the House Select Committee on Assassinations. It investigated the deaths of Kennedy and Dr. Martin Luther

John F. Kennedy

SELECT COMMITTEE ON ASSASSINATIONS
U.S. HOUSE OF REPRESENTATIVES
J.F.K. FIREARMS EXAMINATION

MISCELLANEOUS EVIDENCE WORKSHEET

ITEM NO. *CE 351*

DESCRIPTION: ONE TINTED AUTOMOBILE WINDSHIELD, MEASURING 29 5/16" high × 49 3/4" WIDE AT THE TOP, AND 65 3/4" WIDE AT THE BOTTOM. (ALL MEASUREMENTS MADE AT WIDEST POINTS OF WINDSHIELD). THE WINDSHIELD IS TWO LAYER, LAMINATED GLASS, TINTED, WITH DARKER TINTING AT THE TOP, APPROX THICKNESS .283".

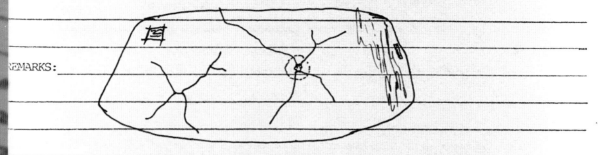

REMARKS:

A POINT OF IMPACT IS LOCATED ON THE INSIDE OF THE WINDSHIELD 13 3/8" BELOW THE TOP EDGE & 22 7/8" TO THE RIGHT OF THE LEFT EDGE. (MEASUREMENTS MADE FROM THE FRONT SIDE) SOME AREAS OF THE IMPACT ON THE OUTSIDE (FRONT) SURFACE ARE CRACKED, INDICATING THAT THE FORCE (DIRECTION) OF IMPACT OCCURRED ON THE INSIDE OF THE WINDSHIELD. ALSO, THERE IS ANOTHER SERIES OF CRACKS ON THE RIGHT SIDE OF THE WINDSHIELD, THAT ARE NOT DIRECTLY CONNECTED TO THOSE RADIATING FROM THE POINT OF IMPACT. THE OUTER EDGES OF THE WINDSHIELD ARE COVERED WITH MASKING TAPE. THE LEFT SIDE OUTER (FRONT) SURFACE HAS DRIED STAINED MATERIAL ADHERING TO IT.   (OVER)

EXAMINERS _____   DATE: _____
           JK Bates Jr.   JUNE 2, 1978

King Jr., who had been killed in 1968. The committee published its report, which it turned in to the House of Representatives in January 1979.

The committee's report said that neither the Secret Service, FBI, CIA, organized crime organizations, nor the Cuban or Soviet governments had conspired to kill Kennedy. The report did not say that individuals from any of these groups could not have done it independently. The committee declared that the Warren Commission's report was well done. It simply stated that it lacked some information.

Both the Warren Commission's and the House Select Committee's reports criticized the Secret Service and the FBI. They felt that the two groups had not done enough to protect the president. The House Select Committee claimed that the Secret Service did not analyze all of the information regarding the president's trip to Dallas. It also felt that the Secret Service did not provide proper protection against possible assassination.

The committee felt that the FBI's investigation was missing information.

The House Select Committee on Assassinations concluded that:

Lee Harvey Oswald fired three shots at President Kennedy.

The second and third shots killed the president.

It was likely that two people fired at President Kennedy.

Scientific evidence went against some conspiracy accusations.

President Kennedy was probably killed as the result of a conspiracy.

U.S. government officials involved in Kennedy's assassination investigation did their jobs with varying degrees of skill.

President Kennedy was not protected as he should have been.

A thorough investigation into Lee Harvey Oswald's role in the killing was conducted.

The investigation into a possible conspiracy was poorly done.

Opposite page: *The House Select Committee re-opened the Kennedy investigation ten years later. They examine evidence such as this report.*

It thought the FBI should have done a more thorough investigation of people involved in organized crime and both pro-Castro and anti-Castro Cubans. It should also have looked closer at anyone from these groups with ties to Lee Harvey Oswald or Jack Ruby. Without this information, the FBI would not have been able to uncover a conspiracy if there would have been one.

There were many holes in the investigation. The FBI did not share all of the information it had gathered with the Warren Commission. It did not tell the commission that several FBI officials had been disciplined for lapses in a security investigation of Oswald before Kennedy was killed. The commission stated that the FBI was not consistent in its investigation of the president's death.

Other departments were lacking as well. Before the Warren Commission was formed, the Department of Justice did nothing to help the FBI's investigation, even though the FBI is part of the department. The FBI, CIA, Department of Justice, and Secret Service all failed to consider a conspiracy in their first investigations into Kennedy's assassination.

President John F. Kennedy was loved by many people. He worked hard for civil rights and to ensure national security against aggressive enemies. He gained tremendous public support throughout his political career. When he was assassinated, people were uncomfortable not knowing who was responsible for killing the promising young president. His assassination was a tragic event in American history.

Opposite page: *Investigators carry the rifle allegedly used to kill Kennedy.*

TIMELINE

1917 John Fitzgerald Kennedy is born.

1940 Kennedy graduates from Harvard University.

1943 Kennedy receives a Purple Heart and the Navy and Marine Corps Medal for heroism.

1946 Kennedy is elected to the House of Representatives. He is elected to two more terms in 1948 and 1950.

1952 Kennedy is elected to the Senate. He is elected to a second Senate term in 1958.

1953 Kennedy marries Jacqueline Bouvier.

1955 Kennedy writes the book *Profiles in Courage*, which wins the Pulitzer Prize in 1957.

1961   Kennedy is sworn in as president of the United States.

The United States invades Cuba at the Bay of Pigs.

Kennedy and Soviet leader Nikita Khrushchev meet
in Vienna, Austria.

The Berlin wall is built in Germany.

1962   The United States faces the Cuban missile crisis.

1963   Kennedy is assassinated on November 22.

Lyndon B. Johnson is sworn in as president on
November 22 aboard *Air Force One*.

Lee Harvey Oswald is arrested on November 22 for
Kennedy's assassination.

Jack Ruby kills Oswald on November 24.

1967   Jack Ruby dies in prison of cancer.

*American
Moments*

FAST FACTS

John F. Kennedy wrote two books. His first book, *Why England Slept*, became a best seller. His second book, *Profiles in Courage*, won the Pulitzer Prize for biography in 1957.

John Kennedy held several political posts. He was elected to three terms as state representative and two terms as senator before serving one term as president of the United States.

Kennedy was the United States's first Roman Catholic president.

Jackie Kennedy redecorated the White House to reflect the richness of U.S. history. She led a videotaped tour of the White House. It was broadcast on television around the world on February 14, 1962.

President Kennedy created a civil rights bill in 1963, which was passed after his death.

President Kennedy and Governor John B. Connally were shot on November 22, 1963, in Dallas, Texas. The president was trying to gain support from Southerners for his reelection the following year.

Lyndon B. Johnson was sworn in as president on November 22, 1963, aboard the presidential airplane, *Air Force One*.

Conspiracy theories surrounding Kennedy's assassination question whether the mafia, the U.S. government, or the governments of Cuba or the Soviet Union were involved. No evidence has been found to incriminate anyone in these groups.

WEB SITES
WWW.ABDOPUB.COM

Would you like to learn more about the assassination of John F. Kennedy? Please visit **www.abdopub.com** to find up-to-date Web site links about the assassination of John F. Kennedy and other American moments. These links are routinely monitored and updated to provide the most current information available.

Guards escort Lee Harvey Oswald two days after his arrest.

GLOSSARY

anonymous: without giving or having a name.

campaign: to give speeches and state ideas in order to be voted into an elected office.

communism: a social and economic system in which everything is owned by the government and is distributed to the people as needed.

conspiracy: a secret agreement between two or more people to commit an unlawful or wrongful act.

court-martial: a trial by a military court for members of the armed forces.

Democratic: a major political party in the United States. It is also a type of government that is led by the people through elected representatives.

Department of Justice: the department in charge of enforcing federal laws.

desegregation: to make it against the law to separate people: in U.S. history it stopped the separation of African Americans and whites in schools and other public places.

electoral vote: the votes given to each state based on the number of senators and representatives it has in Congress.

exile: a person who has been sent away from his or her home country by law or decree.

House of Representatives: the lower house in the U.S. Congress. Citizens elect members of the house to make laws for the nation.

inauguration: a ceremony in which a person is sworn into office.

incumbent: the person currently holding a political office.

malaria: a disease that causes chills, fever, and sweating. It is passed to humans by mosquitoes.

motorcade: a parade of vehicles.

national convention: a national meeting held every four years by members of a political party to choose a presidential candidate.

pallbearer: someone who helps carry the casket at a funeral.

popular vote: the actual number of citizens' votes a candidate receives.

primary election: an early election in which registered voters of a political party choose which candidates will represent their party in the upcoming election.

propaganda: information that is given out to support a particular idea or belief.

Pulitzer Prize: an award established by Joseph Pulitzer for accomplishments in journalism, literature, drama, and music.

Republican: one of two major political parties in the United States.

Secret Service: a government agency in charge of protecting the president.

Senate: the upper house of the U.S. Congress. Citizens elect members of the Senate to make laws for the nation.

INDEX